An Animal Family

SHARKS AND PUPS

By Natalie Humphrey

Gareth Stevens
PUBLISHING

Please visit our website, www.garethstevens.com. For a free color catalog of all our high-quality books, call toll free 1-800-542-2595 or fax 1-877-542-2596.

Library of Congress Cataloging-in-Publication Data

Names: Humphrey, Natalie, author.
Title: Sharks and pups / Natalie Humphrey.
Description: New York : Gareth Stevens Publishing, [2021] | Series: An animal family | Includes index.
Identifiers: LCCN 2019045216 | ISBN 9781538255926 (library binding) | ISBN 9781538255902 (paperback) | ISBN 9781538255919 (6 pack)| ISBN 9781538255933 (ebook)
Subjects: LCSH: Sharks–Infancy–Juvenile literature. | Sharks–Development–Juvenile literature.
Classification: LCC QL638.9 .H86 2021 | DDC 597.3/31392–dc23
LC record available at https://lccn.loc.gov/2019045216

First Edition

Published in 2021 by
Gareth Stevens Publishing
111 East 14th Street, Suite 349
New York, NY 10003

Editor: Natalie Humphrey
Designer: Katelyn E. Reynolds

Photo credits: Cover, pp. 1, 23 Ken Kiefer 2/Image Source/Getty Images; p. 5 Shane Gross/Shutterstock.com; p. 7 Federica Grassi/Moment/Getty Images; p. 9 Anita Kainrath/Shutterstock.com; p. 11 Vagabondivan/Shutterstock.com; p. 13 Andrea Izzotti/Shutterstock.com; pp. 15, 24 (mermaid purse) Tatjana Kabanova/Shutterstock.com; p. 17 Michael Bogner/Shutterstock.com; pp. 19, 24 (fish) Westend61/India/Getty Images; p. 21 Krzysztof Bargiel/Shutterstock.com.

Printed in the United States of America

CPSIA compliance information: Batch #CS20GS: For further information contact Gareth Stevens, New York, New York at 1-800-542-2595.

Contents

Pups on Their Own 4
Lots of Pups 10
Growing up Alone 20
Words to Know 24
Index. 24

A pup is a baby shark.

Sharks don't raise their babies.

Mothers find a safe spot.
They leave the pups alone.

Sharks can be born live.

Some sharks lay eggs.

They are called mermaid purses.

Sharks have
a lot of pups.
They can have
up to 100!

Pups are small.
They eat fish.

They are very fast.
They hide from danger.

Pups are slow growers. It can take 18 years to grow up!

Words to Know

fish

mermaid purse

Index

baby 4, 6
mother 8
egg 12
year 22